VEGETATION ZONES

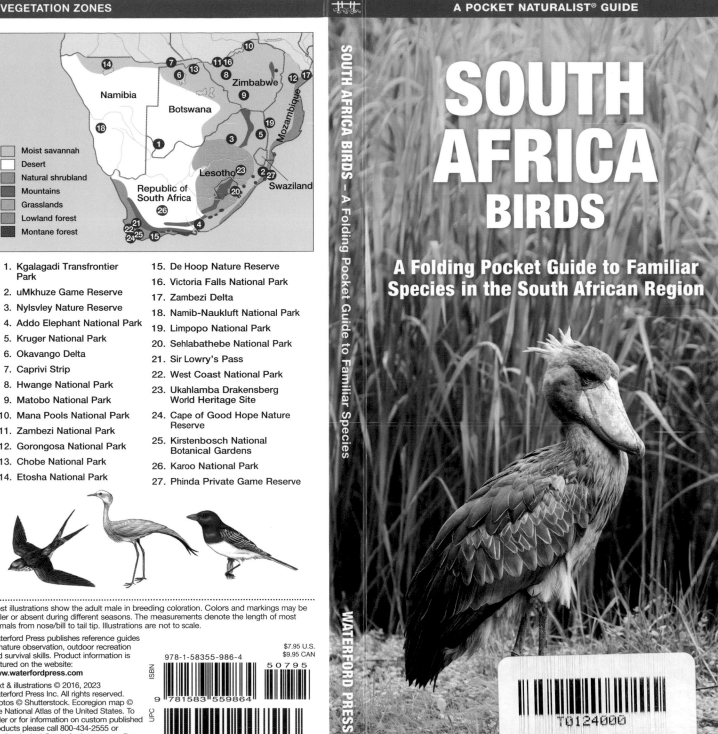

Namibia

Botswana

Zimbabwe

Mozambique

Namibia

Lesotho

Republic of South Africa

Swaziland

Moist savannah
Desert
Natural shrubland
Mountains
Grasslands
Lowland forest
Montane forest

1. Kgalagadi Transfrontier Park
2. uMkhuze Game Reserve
3. Nylsvley Nature Reserve
4. Addo Elephant National Park
5. Kruger National Park
6. Okavango Delta
7. Caprivi Strip
8. Hwange National Park
9. Matobo National Park
10. Mana Pools National Park
11. Zambezi National Park
12. Gorongosa National Park
13. Chobe National Park
14. Etosha National Park
15. De Hoop Nature Reserve
16. Victoria Falls National Park
17. Zambezi Delta
18. Namib-Naukluft National Park
19. Limpopo National Park
20. Sehlabathebe National Park
21. Sir Lowry's Pass
22. West Coast National Park
23. Ukhahlamba Drakensberg World Heritage Site
24. Cape of Good Hope Nature Reserve
25. Kirstenbosch National Botanical Gardens
26. Karoo National Park
27. Phinda Private Game Reserve

Waterford Press publishes reference guides to nature observation, outdoor recreation and survival skills. Product information is featured on the website:
www.waterfordpress.com

Text & illustrations © 2016, 2023 Waterford Press Inc. All rights reserved. Photos © Shutterstock. Ecoregion map © The National Atlas of the United States. To order or for information on custom published products please call 800-434-2555 or email orderdesk@waterfordpress.com. For permissions or to share comments email editor@waterfordpress.com. 2311322

$7.95 U.S.
$9.95 CAN

978-1-58355-986-4

ISBN

50779 5
9 781583 559864
UPC
8 44682 00755 3
10 9 8 7 6 5 4 3 2 1
Made in the USA

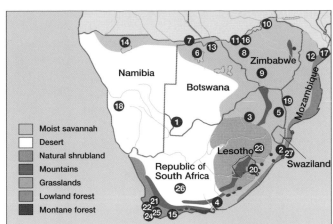

SOUTH AFRICA BIRDS

A Folding Pocket Guide to Familiar Species in the South African Region

SOUTH AFRICA BIRDS – A Folding Pocket Guide to Familiar Species

WATERFORD PRESS

T0124000

Jackass Penguin
Spheniscus demersus
To 28 in. (70 cm)
Breeds on islands off south and west coast.

Red-billed Teal
Anas erythrorhyncha
To 20 in. (50 cm)
The similar cape teal has a gray head.

Dabchick
Tachybaptus ruficollis
To 12 in. (30 cm)
Also called little grebe.

Spur-winged Goose
Plectropterus gambensis
To 40 in. (1 m)
Note pinkish knob on forehead.

Egyptian Goose
Alopochen aegyptiaca
To 30 in. (75 cm)
Note reddish patch around orange eye.

African Darter
Anhinga rufa
To 3 ft. (90 cm)
Found on inland lakes and waterways.

African Pygmy Goose
Nettapus auritus
To 13 in. (33 cm)

Yellow-billed Duck
Anas undulata To 23 in. (58 cm)
Note dark saddle on yellow bill.

White-faced Duck
Dendrocygna viduata
To 20 in. (50 cm)

Reed Cormorant
Phalacrocorax africanus
To 20 in. (50 cm)
Note long tail and red eye.

Cape Cormorant
Phalacrocorax capensis
To 26 in. (65 cm)
Note orange face patch.

White-breasted Cormorant
Phalacrocorax lucidus
To 40 in. (1 m)

Red Knot
Calidris canutus
To 12 in. (30 cm)
Plump, red-breasted shorebird.

Sanderling
Calidris alba
To 8 in. (20 cm)
Runs in and out with waves along shorelines.

Winter

Ruddy Turnstone
Arenaria interpres
To 10 in. (25 cm)

Cattle Egret
Bubulcus ibis
To 20 in. (50 cm)

Little Egret
Egretta garzetta
To 26 in. (65 cm)
Note black bill and yellow feet.

Great Egret
Ardea alba
To 38 in. (95 cm)
Note yellow bill and black feet.

Gray Heron
Ardea cinerea
To 38 in. (95 cm)

Squacco Heron
Ardeola ralloides
To 16 in. (40 cm)
White wings are conspicuous in flight.

Great White Pelican
Pelecanus onocrotalus
To 5.5 ft. (1.7 m)
The similar pink-backed pelican is smaller and has a pinkish bill.

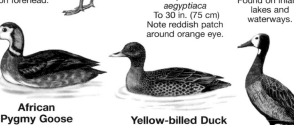

Black-crowned Night-Heron
Nycticorax nycticorax
To 28 in. (70 cm)

Green-backed Heron
Butorides striatus
To 14 in. (35 cm)
Note black cap.

Black-headed Heron
Ardea melanocephala
To 40 in. (1 m)

Hammerkop
Scopus umbretta
To 22 in. (55 cm)
Head is hammer-shaped.

Blacksmith Plover
Vanellus armatus
To 12 in. (30 cm)
Named for its call – klink, klink – which sounds like a hammer on an anvil.

Crowned Plover
Vanellus coronatus
To 12 in. (30 cm)
Black cap is encircled by a white ring.

Three-banded Plover
Charadrius tricollaris
To 8 in. (20 cm)
Note red eye ring.

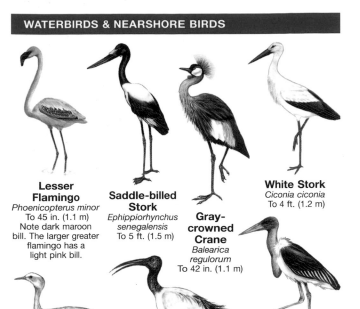

Lesser Flamingo
Phoenicopterus minor
To 45 in. (1.1 m)
Note dark maroon bill. The larger greater flamingo has a light pink bill.

Saddle-billed Stork
Ephippiorhynchus senegalensis
To 5 ft. (1.5 m)

Gray-crowned Crane
Balearica regulorum
To 42 in. (1.1 m)

White Stork
Ciconia ciconia
To 4 ft. (1.2 m)

Blue Crane
Anthropoides paradisea
To 42 in. (1.1 m)
South Africa's national bird.

Marabou Stork
Leptoptilos crumeniferus
To 5 ft. (1.5 m)
Scavenging bird competes with vultures for carrion.

Sacred Ibis
Threskiornis aethiopica
To 3 ft. (90 cm)

African Spoonbill
Platalea alba
To 3 ft. (90 cm)
Bill has a spoon-shaped tip.

Hadeda Ibis
Bostrychia hagedash
To 3 ft. (90 cm)
Note red mark on bill and white facial crescent. Call is a loud – ha-de-dah.

Black-capped Avocet
Recurvirostra avosetta
To 18 in. (45 cm)

African Black Oystercatcher
Haematopus moquini
To 20 in. (50 cm)

Ruff
Philomachus pugnax
To 12 in. (30 cm)

Black-winged Stilt
Himantopus himantopus
To 15 in. (38 cm)

African Black Crake
Amaurornis flavirostris
To 8 in. (20 cm)
Note red legs and yellow bill.

Red-knobbed Coot
Fulica cristata
To 18 in. (45 cm)
Two red forehead knobs are prominent during breeding season.

African Jacana
Actophilornis africana
To 12 in. (30 cm)
Long-toed swamp bird walks on the floating leaves of waterplants.

Purple Gallinule
Porphyrio martinicus
To 13 in. (33 cm)

Cape Gannet
Morus capensis
To 40 in. (1 m)

Gray-headed Gull
Chroicocephalus cirrocephalus
To 18 in. (45 cm)

Common Moorhen
Gallinula chloropus
To 14 in. (35 cm)
Note white stripe on flank.

Kelp Gull
Larus dominicanus
To 2 ft. (60 cm)

White-winged Tern
Chlidonias leucopterus
To 9 in. (23 cm)

QUAIL, OSTRICH, ETC.

Red-necked Francolin
Francolinus afer
To 14 in. (35 cm)

Ostrich
Struthio camelus
To 9 ft. (2.7 m)
One of the world's heaviest flying birds. The smaller black bustard has a black head, neck and undersides and a white ear patch.

Kori Bustard
Choriotis kori
To 52 in. (1.3 m)
One of the world's heaviest and heaviest flightless bird on earth.

Helmeted Guineafowl
Numida meleagris
To 22 in. (55 cm)

Common Quail
Coturnix coturnix
To 7 in. (18 cm)
Note streaked pattern on face.

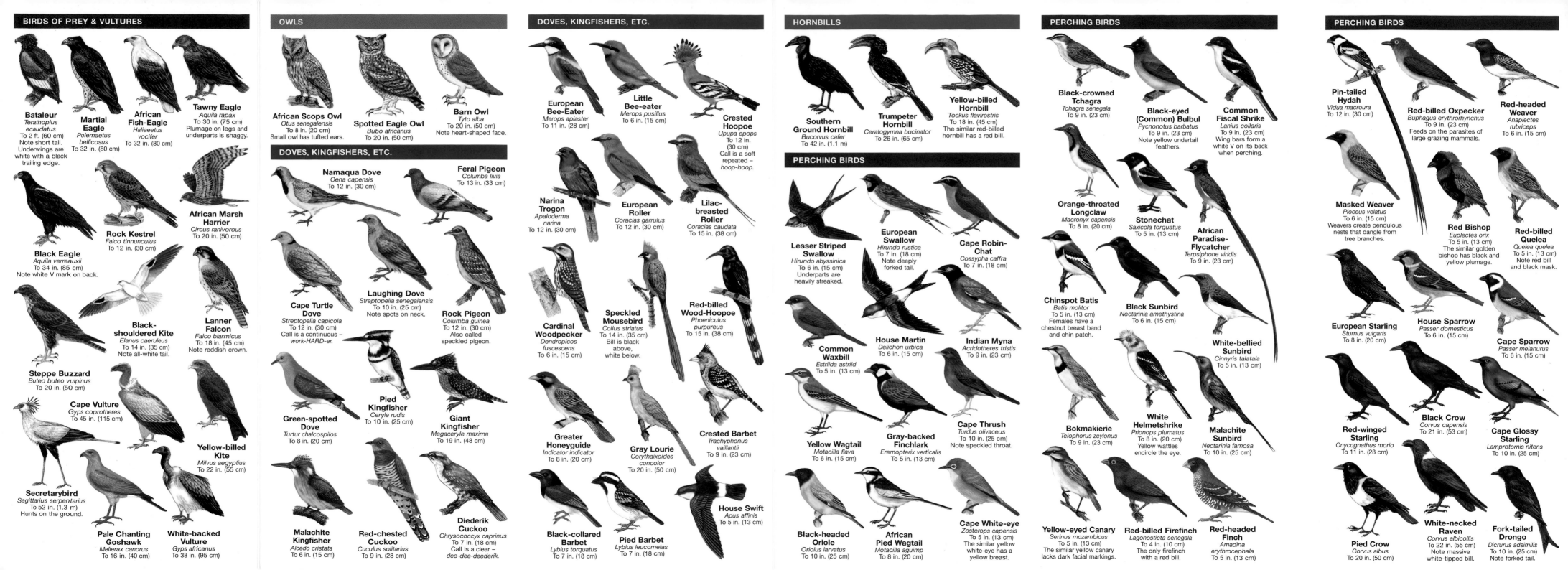

BIRDS OF PREY & VULTURES

Bataleur
Terathopius ecaudatus
To 2 ft. (60 cm)
Note short tail.
Underwings are
white with a black
trailing edge.

Martial Eagle
Polemaetus bellicosus
To 32 in. (80 cm)

African Fish-Eagle
Haliaeetus vocifer
To 32 in. (80 cm)

Tawny Eagle
Aquila rapax
To 30 in. (75 cm)
Plumage on legs and
underparts is shaggy.

Rock Kestrel
Falco tinnunculus
To 12 in. (30 cm)

African Marsh Harrier
Circus ranivorous
To 20 in. (50 cm)

Black Eagle
Aquila verreauxii
To 34 in. (85 cm)
Note white V mark on back.

Black-shouldered Kite
Elanus caeruleus
To 14 in. (35 cm)
Note all-white tail.

Lanner Falcon
Falco biarmicus
To 18 in. (45 cm)
Note reddish crown.

Steppe Buzzard
Buteo buteo vulpinus
To 20 in. (50 cm)

Cape Vulture
Gyps coprotheres
To 45 in. (115 cm)

Yellow-billed Kite
Milvus aegyptius
To 22 in. (55 cm)

Secretarybird
Sagittarius serpentarius
To 52 in. (1.3 m)
Hunts on the ground.

Pale Chanting Goshawk
Melierax canorus
To 16 in. (40 cm)

White-backed Vulture
Gyps africanus
To 38 in. (95 cm)

OWLS

African Scops Owl
Otus senegalensis
To 8 in. (20 cm)
Small owl has tufted ears.

Spotted Eagle Owl
Bubo africanus
To 20 in. (50 cm)

Barn Owl
Tyto alba
To 20 in. (50 cm)
Note heart-shaped face.

DOVES, KINGFISHERS, ETC.

Namaqua Dove
Oena capensis
To 12 in. (30 cm)

Feral Pigeon
Columba livia
To 13 in. (33 cm)

Cape Turtle Dove
Streptopelia capicola
To 12 in. (30 cm)
Call is a continuous –
work-HARD-er.

Laughing Dove
Streptopelia senegalensis
To 10 in. (25 cm)
Note spots on neck.

Rock Pigeon
Columba guinea
To 12 in. (30 cm)
Also called
speckled pigeon.

Green-spotted Dove
Turtur chalcospilos
To 8 in. (20 cm)

Pied Kingfisher
Ceryle rudis
To 10 in. (25 cm)

Giant Kingfisher
Megaceryle maxima
To 19 in. (48 cm)

Malachite Kingfisher
Alcedo cristata
To 6 in. (15 cm)

Red-chested Cuckoo
Cuculus solitarius
To 9 in. (28 cm)

Diederik Cuckoo
Chrysococcyx caprinus
To 7 in. (18 cm)
Call is a clear –
dee-dee-dederik.

DOVES, KINGFISHERS, ETC.

European Bee-Eater
Merops apiaster
To 11 in. (28 cm)

Little Bee-eater
Merops pusillus
To 6 in. (15 cm)

Crested Hoopoe
Upupa epops
To 12 in. (30 cm)
Call is a soft
repeated –
hoop-hoop.

Narina Trogon
Apaloderma narina
To 12 in. (30 cm)

European Roller
Coracias garrulus
To 12 in. (30 cm)

Lilac-breasted Roller
Coracias caudata
To 15 in. (38 cm)

Cardinal Woodpecker
Dendropicos fuscescens
To 6 in. (15 cm)

Speckled Mousebird
Colius striatus
To 14 in. (35 cm)
Bill is black
above,
white below.

Red-billed Wood-Hoopoe
Phoeniculus purpureus
To 15 in. (38 cm)

Greater Honeyguide
Indicator indicator
To 8 in. (20 cm)

Gray Lourie
Corythaixoides concolor
To 20 in. (50 cm)

Crested Barbet
Trachyphonus vaillantii
To 9 in. (23 cm)

Black-collared Barbet
Lybius torquatus
To 7 in. (18 cm)

Pied Barbet
Lybius leucomelas
To 7 in. (18 cm)

House Swift
Apus affinis
To 5 in. (13 cm)

HORNBILLS

Southern Ground Hornbill
Bucorvus cafer
To 42 in. (1.1 m)

Trumpeter Hornbill
Ceratogymna bucinator
To 26 in. (65 cm)

Yellow-billed Hornbill
Tockus flavirostris
To 18 in. (45 cm)
The similar red-billed
hornbill has a red bill.

PERCHING BIRDS

Lesser Striped Swallow
Hirundo abyssinica
To 6 in. (15 cm)
Underparts are
heavily streaked.

European Swallow
Hirundo rustica
To 7 in. (18 cm)
Note deeply
forked tail.

Cape Robin-Chat
Cossypha caffra
To 7 in. (18 cm)

Common Waxbill
Estrilda astrild
To 5 in. (13 cm)

House Martin
Delichon urbica
To 6 in. (15 cm)

Indian Myna
Acridotheres tristis
To 9 in. (23 cm)

Yellow Wagtail
Motacilla flava
To 6 in. (15 cm)

Gray-backed Finchlark
Eremopterix verticalis
To 5 in. (13 cm)

Cape Thrush
Turdus olivaceus
To 10 in. (25 cm)
Note speckled throat.

Black-headed Oriole
Oriolus larvatus
To 10 in. (25 cm)

African Pied Wagtail
Motacilla aguimp
To 8 in. (20 cm)

Cape White-eye
Zosterops capensis
To 5 in. (13 cm)
The similar yellow
white-eye has a
yellow breast.

PERCHING BIRDS

Black-crowned Tchagra
Tchagra senegala
To 9 in. (23 cm)

Black-eyed (Common) Bulbul
Pycnonotus barbatus
To 9 in. (23 cm)
Note yellow undertail
feathers.

Common Fiscal Shrike
Lanius collaris
To 9 in. (23 cm)
Wing bars form a
white V on its back
when perching.

Orange-throated Longclaw
Macronyx capensis
To 8 in. (20 cm)

Stonechat
Saxicola torquatus
To 5 in. (13 cm)

African Paradise-Flycatcher
Terpsiphone viridis
To 9 in. (23 cm)

Chinspot Batis
Batis molitor
To 5 in. (13 cm)
Females have a
chestnut breast band
and chin patch.

Black Sunbird
Nectarinia amethystina
To 6 in. (15 cm)

White-bellied Sunbird
Cinnyris talatala
To 5 in. (13 cm)

Bokmakierie
Telophorus zeylonus
To 9 in. (23 cm)

White Helmetshrike
Prionops plumatus
To 8 in. (20 cm)
Yellow wattles
encircle the eye.

Malachite Sunbird
Nectarinia famosa
To 10 in. (25 cm)

Yellow-eyed Canary
Serinus mozambicus
To 5 in. (13 cm)
The similar yellow canary
lacks dark facial markings.

Red-billed Firefinch
Lagonosticta senegala
To 4 in. (10 cm)
The only firefinch
with a red bill.

Red-headed Finch
Amadina erythrocephala
To 5 in. (13 cm)

PERCHING BIRDS

Pin-tailed Hydah
Vidua macroura
To 12 in. (30 cm)

Red-billed Oxpecker
Buphagus erythrorhynchus
To 9 in. (23 cm)
Feeds on the parasites of
large grazing mammals.

Red-headed Weaver
Anaplectes rubriceps
To 6 in. (15 cm)

Masked Weaver
Ploceus velatus
To 6 in. (15 cm)
Weavers create pendulous
nests that dangle from
tree branches.

Red Bishop
Euplectes orix
To 5 in. (13 cm)
The similar golden
bishop has black and
yellow plumage.

Red-billed Quelea
Quelea quelea
To 5 in. (13 cm)
Note red bill
and black mask.

European Starling
Sturnus vulgaris
To 8 in. (20 cm)

House Sparrow
Passer domesticus
To 6 in. (15 cm)

Cape Sparrow
Passer melanurus
To 6 in. (15 cm)

Red-winged Starling
Onycognathus morio
To 11 in. (28 cm)

Black Crow
Corvus capensis
To 21 in. (53 cm)

Cape Glossy Starling
Lamprotornis nitens

Pied Crow
Corvus albus

White-necked Raven
Corvus albicollis
To 22 in. (55 cm)
Note massive
white-tipped bill.

Fork-tailed Drongo
Dicrurus adsimilis
To 10 in. (25 cm)